#MOJOtweet

140 Bite-Sized Ideas on How to Get and Keep Mojo

By Marshall Goldsmith
Foreword by Mitchell Levy

Copyright © 2010 by Marshall Goldsmith

All rights reserved. No patent liability is assumed with respect to the use of the information contained herein. Although every precaution has been taken in the preparation of this book, the publisher and author(s) assume no responsibility for errors or omissions. Neither is any liability assumed for damages resulting from the use of the information contained herein.

First Printing: February 2010

Paperback ISBN: 978-1-61699-022-0 (1-61699-022-8)

Place of Publication: Silicon Valley, California USA

Paperback Library of Congress Number: 2010920819

eBook ISBN: 978-1-61699-023-7 (1-61699-023-6)

Trademarks

All terms mentioned in this book that are known to be trademarks or service marks have been appropriately capitalized. Happy About® and its imprint, THINKaha™, cannot attest to the accuracy of this information. Use of a term in this book should not be regarded as affecting the validity of any trademark or service mark.

Warning and Disclaimer

Every effort has been made to make this book as complete and as accurate as possible, but no warranty of fitness is implied. The information provided is on an "as is" basis. The authors and the publisher shall have neither liability nor responsibility to any person or entity with respect to loss or damages arising from the information contained in this book.

Praise for 'MOJO'

"Another thought provoking, practical, and insightful book by Marshall."

Eduardo Castro-Wright, Vice Chairman, Walmart, the world's largest retailer

---

"As soon as I started reading this book, I felt my Mojo rising."

Mark Tercek, CEO Nature Conservancy, former Managing Partner, Goldman Sachs

---

"The insights in 'MOJO' are certain to help people at all stages of their career tap their full potential and live more fulfilling lives."

John Hammergren, CEO, McKesson Corp, winner of the Warren Bennis Award for Leadership

---

"Mojo is elusive, hard to define, at least as old as Homo sapiens...and worth its weight in gold."

Kevin Kelly, CEO, Heidrick and Struggles, the global search and advisory firm

"Thanks to Marshall for providing another wonderful read, with both short-term and longer-term ideas for personal growth."

Teresa Ressel, CEO, UBS Securities LLC, former Chief Financial Officer, U.S. Treasury.

"'MOJO' focuses on that which lies within us, what we do with it, and how others perceive it resonating from us. A wonderful read!"

Alan Hassenfeld, former CEO, Hasbro

Dedication

To Mitchell Levy and Rajesh Setty.

Thank you for creating THINKaha.

Acknowledgments

To **Buddha**, who knew more about human behavior than anyone I have ever met.

Marshall Goldsmith, *@coachgoldsmith*

Why Did I Write This Book?

I wrote this THINKaha book to share what I know with as many people as I can.

I wrote this book to help my readers have happier and more meaningful lives.

Marshall Goldsmith, *@coachgoldsmith*

140 Bite-Sized Ideas on How to Get and Keep Mojo

#MOJO**tweet**

Contents

Foreword by Mitchell Levy 11

Section I
What Is Mojo? 13

Section II
Mojo Vital Ingredients 31

Section III
Key Terms 43

Section IV
The Mojo Paradox 53

Section V
Mojo Building Block #1: Identity 61

Section VI
Mojo Building Block #2: Achievement　　71

Section VII
Mojo Building Block #3: Reputation　　77

Section VIII
Mojo Building Block #4: Acceptance　　87

Section IX
Mojo Killers　　93

Section X
Your Mojo Tool Kit　　101

Section XI
Final Thoughts　　113

About the Author　　119

Foreword by Mitchell Levy

Mojo is that missing ingredient that is between you and your life filled with meaning and happiness. '#MOJOtweet' provides that in bite-sized packages.

Mitchell Levy, Founder and President, HappyAbout, Inc.

140 Bite-Sized Ideas on How to Get and Keep Mojo

Section 1

What Is Mojo?

Mojo happens the moment when we do something that's purposeful, powerful, and positive, and the rest of the world recognizes it. Some people have it naturally, but everyone can get it and keep it by working on it.

1
Neither misery nor emptiness is a desirable option for most human beings!

2
The only person who can define meaning and happiness for you is YOU!

3

We run everything through two filters: short-term satisfaction (or happiness) and long-term benefit (or meaning). Both have value.

4

The million-dollar question: "What is the one quality that differentiates truly successful people from everyone else?"

5

Truly successful people spend a large part of their lives engaging in activities that simultaneously provide meaning and happiness.

6

My definition of Mojo spins off from the great value I attach to finding happiness and meaning in life.

7

Mojo is the moment when you do something that's purposeful, powerful, and positive, and the rest of the world recognizes it.

8

Mojo is that positive spirit toward what you are doing now that starts from the inside and radiates to the outside.

9

Mojo is an expression of the harmony, or lack of harmony, between what you feel inside about your work and what you show on the outside.

10
Your Mojo is apparent when the positive feelings toward what you are doing come from inside you and are evident for others to see.

11
The payoff of having Mojo: more meaning AND more happiness.

12

Mojo is not just for organizational leaders; it's for all of us, and it applies to all aspects of our lives.

13

Mojo: it's infectious. When people pass their positive spirit to us, we feel like passing it back.

140 Bite-Sized Ideas on How to Get and Keep Mojo

14

Mojo comes from inside ourselves as much as it does from what we are doing.

15

People with high Mojo at work tend to have high Mojo at home.

16

Mojo appears in our lives in various guises.

17

The quest for meaning and happiness becomes more challenging, and yet more important than ever.

18

A man who takes more delight in doing his job well, even at the expense of some easy profit, is rich in Mojo. He will never starve.

#MOJO**tweet**

19

A negative spirit starts from the inside and radiates to the outside. People with a negative spirit have Nojo!

20

Professional Mojo is a measure of the skills and attitudes you bring to any activity.

21

Personal Mojo is measured by the benefits that a particular activity gives back to you.

22

Everyone's day requires different skills and produces different levels of Mojo.

23

People with lots of Mojo did not stumble upon their Mojo by accident.

140 Bite-Sized Ideas on How to Get and Keep Mojo

24

We don't change unless we're compelled to change.

25

Optimism is not just a mindset; it's a form of behavior that guides everything we do.

26

We must apply the positive spirit inside us toward what we are doing now and extend it to what other people are doing.

Section II

Mojo Vital Ingredients

The vital ingredients for Mojo are: your identity, your achievements, your reputation, and your acceptance.

27

Mojo Vital Ingredient #1: Your Identity (**Who do you think you are?**)

28

Mojo Vital Ingredient #2: Your Achievements (**What is the value of your accomplishments?**)

29

Mojo Vital Ingredient #3: Your Reputation (***Who do other people think you are?***)

30

Mojo Vital Ingredient #4: Your Acceptance (***What can you change, and what is beyond your control?***)

31

When Mojo fades, the initial cause is often failure to accept what is and get on with life.

#MOJO**tweet**

32

By understanding the impact and interaction of identity, achievement, reputation, and acceptance, you can begin to alter your own Mojo.

33

When measuring your Mojo, do so in the immediate present, not in the recent past or vague future.

34

Your Mojo in the past is over because, for better or worse, you've changed since then.

35

Your future Mojo is impossible to measure because it hasn't happened yet. It's a fantasy, still unreal.

36

To change your Mojo, you may need to either create a new identity for yourself or rediscover an identity that you have lost.

37

Happiness and meaning can't be experienced next week, next month, or next year. They can only be experienced now.

38

Successful professionals love what they are doing when they are doing it. They are finding happiness and meaning in the present.

39

There are no "right" or "wrong" answers. Nobody is handing out grades. Only you know what you're feeling. Only you can score yourself.

40

People who hate what they're doing but paint a convincing picture of positive spirit on the outside are phonies.

41

People who love what they're doing but somehow never show it are doomed to be misunderstood.

140 Bite-Sized Ideas on How to Get and Keep Mojo

Section III

Key Terms

It helps to understand the five qualities that we bring to any activity and the five benefits that we derive from the activity after a job well done.

42

Five qualities that you need to bring to an activity in order to do it well are: motivation, knowledge, ability, confidence, and authenticity.

43

Five benefits you may receive from an activity after doing a job well are: happiness, reward, meaning, learning, and gratitude.

44

Many successful people have a tendency to overestimate their strengths and underestimate their weaknesses.

45

Motivation is when you want to do a great job in an activity (as opposed to just "going through the motions").

46

Knowledge is when you understand what to do and how to do it (as opposed to being unclear on processes or priorities).

47

Ability is when you have the skills needed to do a task well (as opposed to when it does not fit your talents or competencies).

48

Confidence is when you are sure of yourself when performing an activity (as opposed to feeling unsure or insecure).

49

Authenticity is when you are genuine in your level of enthusiasm for engaging in an activity (as opposed to "faking it").

50

Happiness is when being engaged in an activity makes you happy (as opposed to being engaged in something not so stimulating).

51

Reward is when an activity provides material or emotional rewards that are important to you (as opposed to something unrewarding).

52

Meaning is when the results of an activity are meaningful for you (as opposed to activity where there is no sense of fulfillment).

53

Learning is when an activity helps you to learn and grow (as opposed to feeling you are just "treading water").

54

Gratitude is when you feel grateful for being able to do an activity and believe that it is a great use of your time.

140 Bite-Sized Ideas on How to Get and Keep Mojo

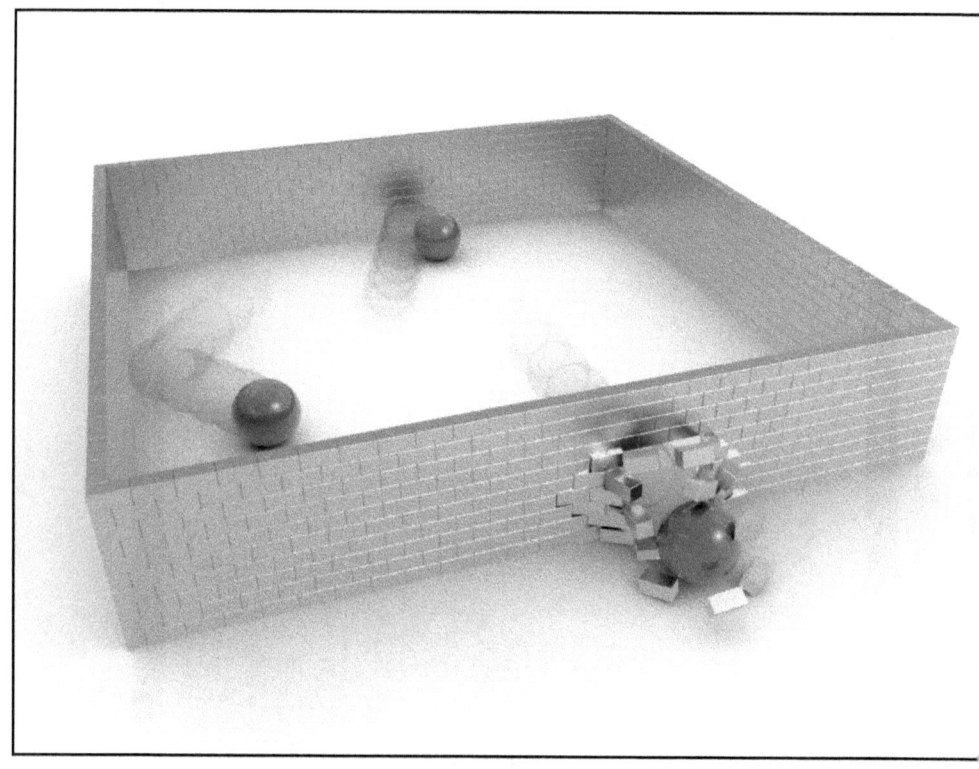

#MOJO**tweet**

Section IV

The Mojo Paradox

Our general tendency is to continue to do what we are already doing, but this might not be sufficient to getting and keeping Mojo.

55

Five key variables emerge with in the Mojo Paradox: health, wealth, relationships, happiness and meaning.

56

Our default response in life is not to experience happiness.

57

Our default response in life is not to experience meaning.

58

Our default response in life is to experience inertia.

59

Quite often inertia is so powerful, the most reliable predictor of what you will be doing five minutes from now is what you are doing now.

#MOJO**tweet**

60

Breaking the cycle is not a matter of exerting heroic willpower. All that's required is the use of a simple discipline.

61

The conclusion is unequivocal. Very few people achieve positive, lasting change without ongoing follow-up.

62

We're more alert to how we behave, perform, and appear to others when we know someone is judging us.

63

Your options are not as limited or limiting as you think. But you may never even consider these options without first posing a few questions.

64

We never have all the information we need; circumstances are rarely perfect.

> #MOJO**tweet**

Section V

Mojo Building Block #1: Identity

You discover your identity by simply answering the question:
Who do you think you are?

65

You don't write a mission statement. You live it and breathe it.

66

When you have a mission, you give yourself a purpose, and that adds clarity to all the actions and decisions that follow.

67

Identity is a complicated subject, and we make it even more complicated when we're not sure where to look for the best answer.

68

The further you go back into your past, the greater the chances that your "Remembered Identity" doesn't match up with who you are today.

69

Identity can cheat you from establishing your Mojo.

70

Even if your "Reflected Identity" is accurate, it doesn't have to be predictive. We can all change!

71

If you change your behavior, but don't change your identity, you may feel "phony" or "unreal," no matter how much you achieve.

72

If you change your behavior and change the way you define yourself, you can be both different and authentic at the same time.

#MOJO**tweet**

73

Your "Created Identity" allows you to become a different person. You can change to fit changing times and to achieve higher goals.

74

Many make the mistake treating identity as a fixed, immutable object. We believe it cannot be altered, at least not significantly.

75

One of the greatest obstacles to changing our Mojo is the paralysis we create with self-limiting definitions of who we are.

76

When we tell ourselves that we can't sell or are awful at speaking in public, we usually find a way to fulfill the prophecy.

77

Our identities are remembered, reflected, programmed, and created.

78

To change your Mojo, you may need to either create a new identity for yourself or rediscover an identity that you have lost.

# Section VI

Mojo Building Block #2: Achievement

You discover your achievements by simply answering the question: **What have you done lately?**

79

Your Personal Mojo is what the activity brings to you.

80

Your Professional Mojo is what you bring to the activity.

81

Both Professional and Personal Mojo are connected to achievement, just two different types of achievement.

82

Achievements make others aware of our ability. It happens every time we do something that's measured or rated by someone else.

83

In many cases, people's self-assessment of how well they do a job is more meaningful to them than what their superiors think.

84

One of the biggest mistakes high achievers make is in overestimating their contribution to a success.

85

If you want to increase your Mojo, you can either change the degree of your achievement or change the definition of your achievement.

86

Influence *up* as well as *down*. Both are important to achieve something significant.

140 Bite-Sized Ideas on How to Get and Keep Mojo

#MOJO**tweet**

Section VII

Mojo Building Block #3: Reputation

You discover your reputation by simply answering the question: **Who do people think you are?**

87

A key element in protecting your reputation is taking "preventative medicine" to ensure it doesn't get damaged.

88

You cannot create your reputation by yourself (the rest of the world always has something to say about it), but you can influence it.

89

We confuse our need to consider ourselves smart with our need to be considered effective by the world.

90

We're so invested in presenting ourselves as smart that we believe we don't need to hear everything that people tell us.

91

After all, what's more frustrating than believing you're smart, yet being powerless to impact a world that believes you are not?

92

Choosing to be effective rather than smart ultimately pays off in your reputation, your achievement, and your Mojo.

93

The connection between your reputation and your Mojo should be self-evident.

94

A negative opinion is usually left unexpressed rather than shared.

95

When other people see a pattern of resemblance, that's when they start forming your reputation.

96

Only when you demonstrate your effectiveness in handling crisis after crisis will your reputation for "shining at crunch time" take shape.

97

One event can't form your reputation. One corrective gesture can't reform your reputation either.

#MOJO**tweet**

98

You need a sequence of consistent, similar actions to begin the rebuilding process of your reputation.

99

Do it right the first time, and you may never have to change your ways.

100

By impacting your reputation you can impact your Mojo.

101

Having a great reputation—in an area that matters in your life—makes Mojo maintenance more of a joy than a chore.

Section VIII

Mojo Building Block #4: Acceptance

You discover acceptance by simply answering the question:
When can you let go?

102

We believe that achieving a goal will somehow make us happy, conveniently ignoring the fact that the goal line always moves slightly beyond our reach.

103

Worrying about the past and being anxious about the future can easily destroy your Mojo.

104

When everything around us seems confusing, acceptance reminds us what really matters.

105

You don't have to like them, agree with them, or even respect them. Just accept them for being who they are.

106

Change what you can and "let go" of what you cannot change.

#MOJO**tweet**

107

Name it. Frame it. Claim it.

140 Bite-Sized Ideas on How to Get and Keep Mojo

Section IX

Mojo Killers

When you have high Mojo, you have more opportunities. That is a good thing, but if you get carried away, that might be what kills your Mojo.

108

Successful people operate in two modes: professional and relaxed.

109

In professional mode, people pay attention to what they say, how they look, whom they must serve, and whom they can't afford to displease.

110

The higher up you are, the bigger the megaphone.

111

Fact: People with high Mojo tend to be assaulted with opportunities. This happens at all levels, high and low.

112

Don't overcommit. Before replying with an enthusiastic "yes" to that next request, think of the long-term impact on your Mojo.

113

The key question to ask all the time: **What path would I take if I knew that the situation would not get better?**

114

While our minds need order and fairness, much of life is neither fair nor just. That's a problem for many of us and is a Mojo killer.

115

Sometimes even achieving a desired level of success can be a sunk cost that limits your Mojo.

116

You had to invest a big piece of yourself in your work. That "investment" may have stopped paying off without you being aware of it.

140 Bite-Sized Ideas on How to Get and Keep Mojo

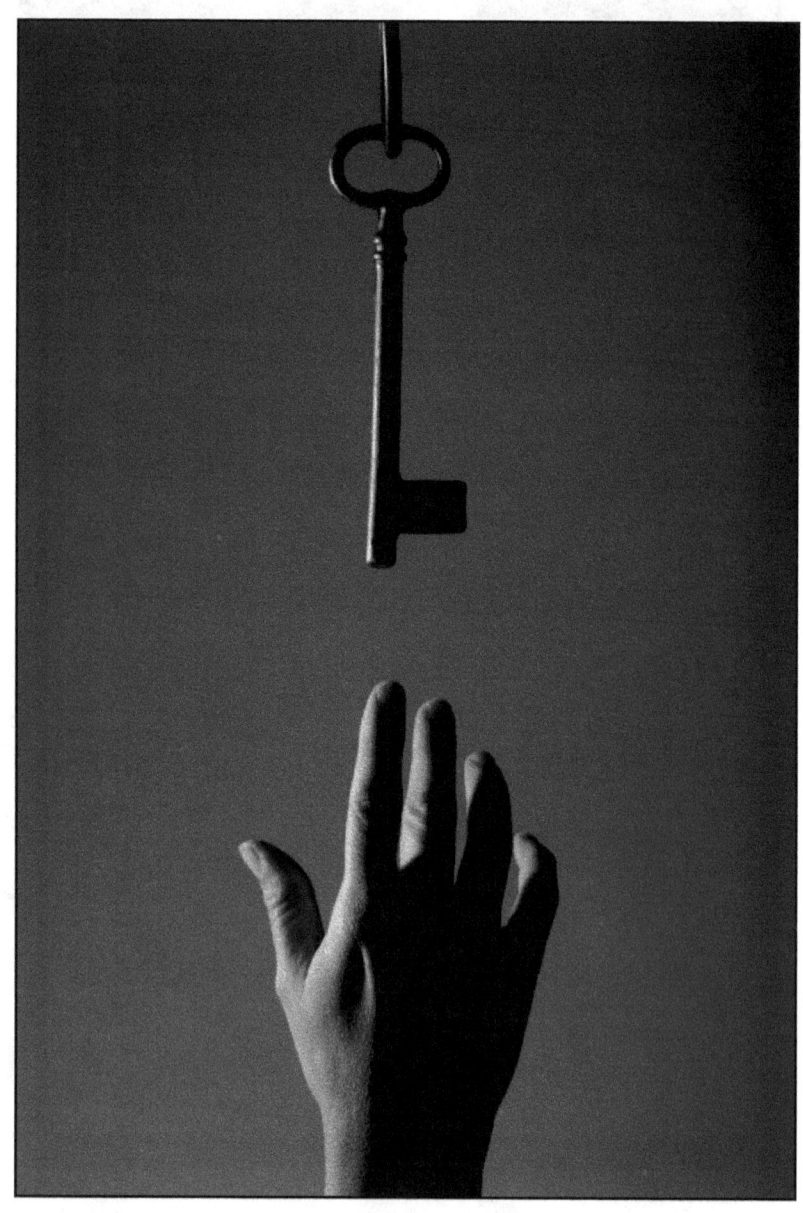

Section X

Your Mojo Tool Kit

Getting and keeping Mojo is not an overnight activity. But you can get it and keep it, brick-by-brick.

117

Mojo is a function of the relationship between who you are (e.g., You) and your situation (e.g., It).

118

What can you change? The answer is simple: you can change either You or It.

119

Changing You is not inherently preferable or easier than changing It (and vice versa). The best approach depends on the situation.

120

It is your life. If your Mojo is suffering, no one can make the "You vs. It" decision for you.

121

You assess a low-Mojo situation and change something fundamental about... It.

122

Mojo Tools: They don't work unless you grab them in your hands and use them.

123

Setting ground rules for your life can start you on the path toward great Mojo.

124

"Where you are headed" is determined by how you balance short-term satisfaction and long-term benefit, at work and at home.

125

There's power in "going for it" and not being afraid to look foolish.

126

A wall is built one brick at a time. So's your Mojo.

127

The small moments in our lives can make big statements about who we are.

128

Live your mission in the small moments too. When to stay, when to go? It's better to jump than be pushed.

129

Swim in the blue water. A new way to win can be to change the game!

#MOJO**tweet**

130

Reduce this number: the percentage of time you spend on boasting about or criticizing yourself and others.

131

Influence **up** as well as **down**: turn important decision makers into your best customers.

132

Name It. Frame It. Claim It. Naming what we do can help us enhance how we do it.

133

Give your friends a lifetime pass. Friends can be more forgiving than we deserve—give them a break.

140 Bite-Sized Ideas on How to Get and Keep Mojo

Section XI

Final Thoughts

Your Mojo is your ticket to a happier and more meaningful life. Here are a few parting thoughts on your journey.

134

Don't panic when you are new, yet don't get lost in your own ego.

135

This is how success happens: a lot of know-how abetted by a little know-who.

136

Communication has a distinct and specific quality; it's either poisonous or drenched in ego. Neither is good for Mojo.

137

For employees who lack Mojo, the world of work can begin to resemble a "new-age professional hell."

138

In this new world, Mojo is both harder to attain and more important to keep.

139

The focus has always been on shaping a happier, more confident, more engaged you.

140 Bite-Sized Ideas on How to Get and Keep Mojo

140

Don't let your ego block you from your goals.

About the Author

Dr. Marshall Goldsmith is a world authority in helping successful leaders get even better by achieving positive, lasting change in behavior: for themselves, their people, and their teams.

His book 'What Got You Here Won't Get You There' is a **New York Times** best seller, **Wall Street Journal** #1 business book, and winner of the Harold Longman award for Best Business Book of the Year. It has been translated into twenty-eight languages and is a listed best seller in seven major countries.

Dr. Goldsmith's Ph.D. is from UCLA. He teaches executive education at Dartmouth's Tuck School and frequently speaks at leading business schools. He is a Fellow of the National Academy of Human Resources (America's top HR honor), and his work has been recognized by almost every professional organization in his field. In 2006, Alliant International University honored Marshall by naming their schools of business and organizational studies, the Marshall Goldsmith School of Management.

Dr. Goldsmith is one of a select few advisors who have been asked to work with over 120 major CEOs and their management teams. He served on the Board of the Peter Drucker Foundation for ten years. He has been a volunteer teacher for U.S. Army Generals, Navy Admirals, Girl Scout executives, and leaders of both the International and American Red Cross, for whom he was a National Volunteer of the Year.

Marshall's twenty-seven books include: 'The Leader of the Future' (a ***BusinessWeek*** best seller); 'The Organization of the Future 2' (Choice Award—top fifteen outstanding academic business books 2009); 'Coaching for Leadership'; and his recently-published ***Wall Street Journal*** best seller, 'Succession: Are You Ready?'

Over three hundred of his articles, interviews, columns, and videos are available for viewing and sharing online at http://www.MarshallGoldsmithLibrary.com. Visitors to this site have come from 195 countries and have viewed, read, listened to, downloaded, or shared resources over 4 million times.

www.ingramcontent.com/pod-product-compliance
Lightning Source LLC
Chambersburg PA
CBHW070052120426
42742CB00048B/2462